Pals

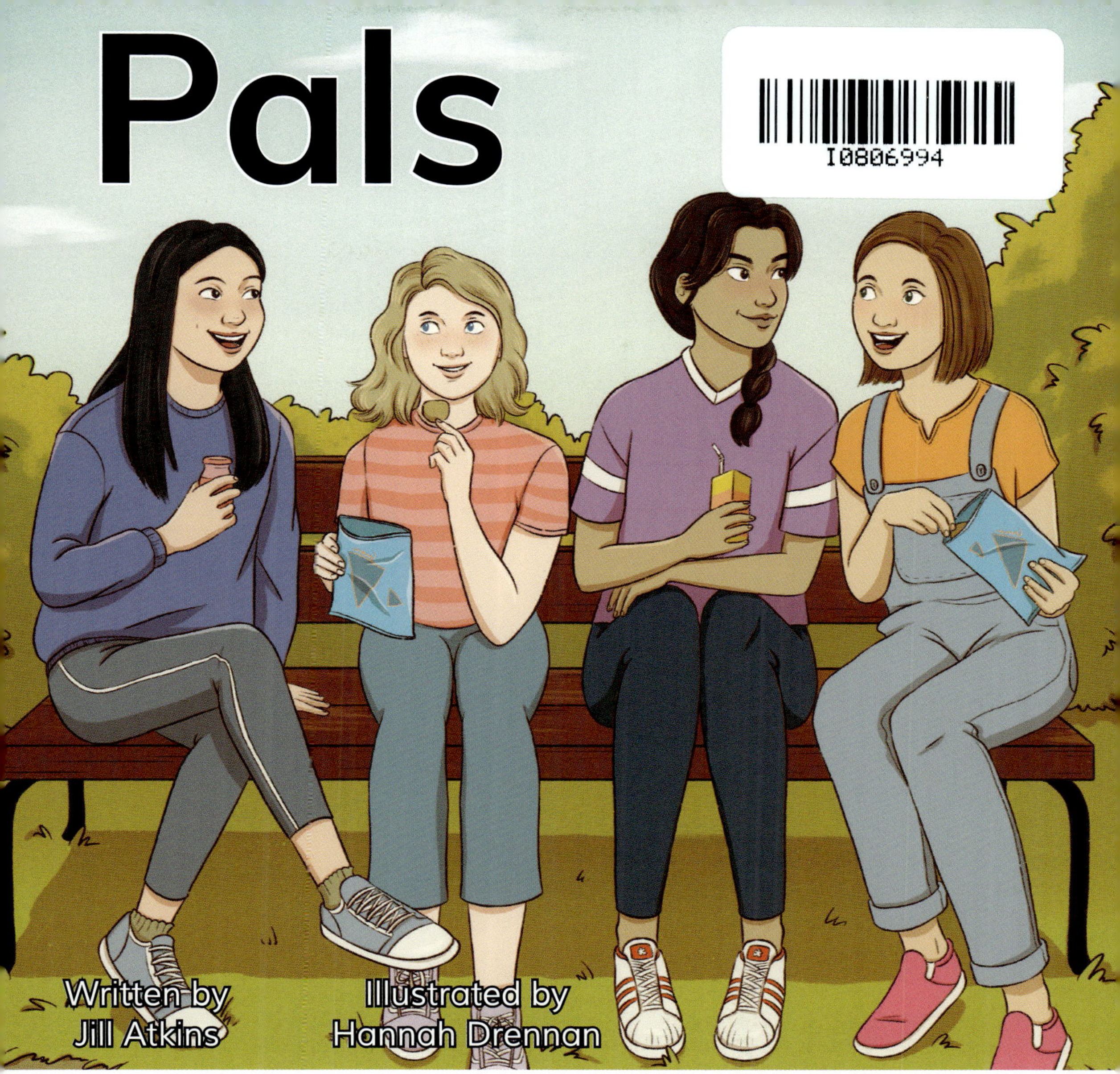

Written by
Jill Atkins

Illustrated by
Hannah Drennan

Published in 2026 by
Norwood House Press
2544 Clinton Street
Buffalo, NY 14224

Printed in the United States of Americc

Library of Congress Cataloging-in-Publication Data:
Names: Atkins, Jill (Children's author). | Jones, Cath, 1965-, author. | Drennan, Hannah, illustrator. | Barr, Ryan, illustrator.
Title: Pals / written by Jill Atkins, illustrated by Hannah Drennan. Jump cap power / written by Cath Jones, illustrated by Ryan Barr.
Description: Buffalo, NY : Norwood House Press, 2026. | Series: Phonics all-stars: phase 4 |
Identifiers: ISBN 9781978578500 (pbk.) | ISBN 9781978578517 (library bound) | ISBN 9781978578524 (ebook)
Subjects: LCSH: Reading–Phonetic method–Juvenile fiction. | English language–Phonetics–Juvenile fiction. | Friendship–Juvenile fiction. | Girls--Juvenile fiction. |
Skateboarding–Juvenile fiction. | Skateboarding parks–Juvenile fiction. | Hats–Juvenile fiction.
Classification: LCC LB1573.3 A796 2026 | DDC 372.465–dc23

CPSIA compliance information: Batch #CW26NHP: For further information contact Norwood House Press at 1-800-237-9932.

That morning, Amber went up to Yasmin.

"My jacket is the best," she said with a grin. "It cost loads."

"Did it?" said Yasmin.

SWIM
MEET

Next morning, Amber went up to Kim.

"Look at my hair," she said. "I bet you wish you had long, black hair too!"

"No," said Kim.

The next week, Amber went to the pool.

"I can swim much better than you," she said to Fran.

Then Amber swam off.

At noon, Amber sat down on a bench to have her lunch.

She felt sad. She had no pal to sit with.

She had too much food in her lunch box.

Kim, Yasmin, and Fran sat on the bench next to Amber.

It was fun to meet and have lunch.

Amber got up and went to sit with them.

"Can I join you?" she said.

She held up her lunch box for them to see.

They sat with Amber and they all had lunch from her lunch box.

"Thank you," said Kim.

"This looks good," said Yasmin.

"Shall we be pals?" said Fran.

"Yes!" said Amber with a grin.

Amber felt good. It was good to have pals.

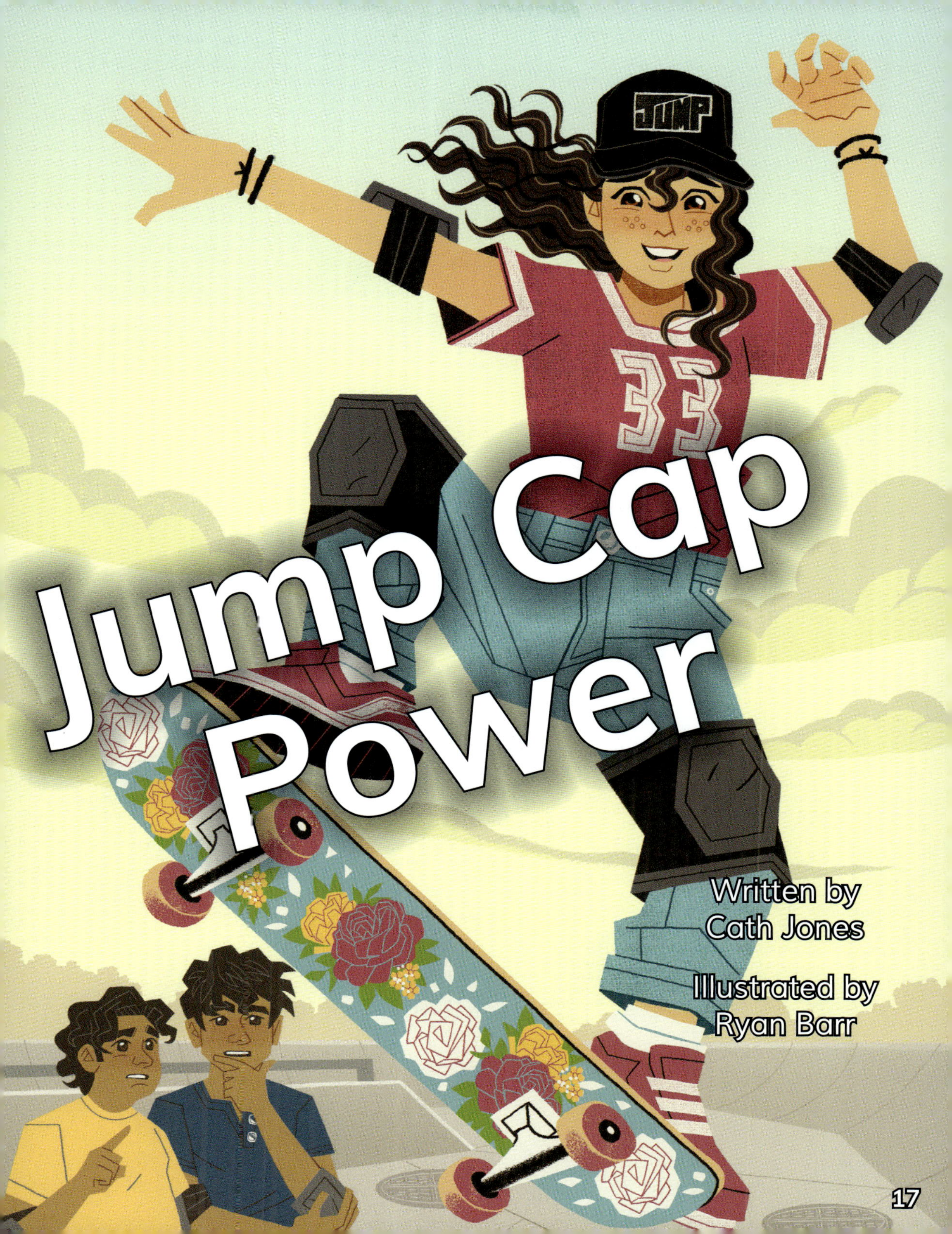

Jump Cap Power

Written by
Cath Jones

Illustrated by
Ryan Barr

I am good at tricks, Anam. Look! I can do a kick flip.
That *is* a good flip, Adeel.

JUMP
Do you like my black **Jump** cap? I can do the best tricks with this cap on.
33

Then Adeel lost his **Jump** cap.

I need my cap, Anam. I cannot do tricks with no cap!

So Adeel and Anam set off
to hunt for the missing cap.

The **Jump** cap was not on the bench.

JUMP
33
Adeel, look! She can do fantastic tricks, just like you!
Yes – and she has a **Jump** cap just like the cap I lost!

I am Adeel. You can do cool tricks.
That is a fantastic **Jump** cap.
Adeel had a **Jump** cap just like that, but he lost it.

I am Kaja.
This **Jump** cap was under the bench. It must be Adeel's.
JUMP

JUMP
Thank you, Kaja! It *is* my cap!

I was so bad at tricks.
But, with the cap on, I am good. With the cap on, I can do the best tricks.

I think the cap has a gift. It has **Jump** cap power!

See if you
can do the best
tricks now ...
JUMP

I can!

So was it the **Jump** cap? Or was it me?
JUMP